D0823059

For Married Men Only
Three Principles for
Loving Your Wife

Tony Evans

MOODY PUBLISHERS
CHICAGO

Scripture quotations are taken from the *New American Standard Bible®*, Copyright © 1960, 1962, 1963, 1968, 1971, 1972, 1973, 1975, 1977, 1995 by The Lockman Foundation. Used by permission. (www.Lockman.org)

All websites listed herein are accurate at the time of publication, but may change in the future or cease to exist. The listing of website references and resources does not imply publisher endorsement of the site's entire contents. Groups, corporations, and organizations are listed for informational purposes, and listing does not imply publisher endorsement of their activities.

Editor: Christopher Reese
Interior Design: Ragont Design
Cover Design: John Hamilton Design
Cover Image: iStock

Library of Congress Cataloging-in-Publication Data

Evans, Tony, 1949-
 For married men only : three principles to ignite love / Tony Evans.
    p. cm.
 ISBN 978-0-8024-4382-3
1. Husbands--Religious life. 2. Marriage--Religious
aspects--Christianity. I. Title.
 BV4528.3.E93 2010
 248.8'425--dc22

                                    2010007600

We hope you enjoy this book from Moody Publishers. Our goal is to provide high-quality, thought-provoking books and products that connect truth to your real needs and challenges. For more information on other books and products written and produced from a biblical perspective, go to www.moodypublishers.com or write to:

Moody Publishers
820 N. LaSalle Boulevard
Chicago, IL 60610

7 9 10 8 6

Printed in the United States of America

CONTENTS

1

THE ROLE OF SAVIOR

A preacher was performing a wedding when he came to the part of the ceremony in which it is traditional to ask if anyone present knows any reason why the wedding should not proceed. So the preacher asked if there was anyone who objected to this marriage, and a voice rang out through the church, "I do."

"Quiet," the preacher said. "You're the groom. You can't object!"

I've never conducted a wedding in which this has happened. But judging by the staggering divorce statistics in our culture, maybe there should be more wedding ceremonies that are brought to a halt because someone objects to the union. And that includes weddings between two Christians, because the body of Christ in

America isn't doing any better than the world when it comes to divorce.

It's obvious that a lot of people are getting married with little or no idea of what they're doing and/or with a faulty view of the person they are marrying. We all know that during the courting process a lot of selling goes on. Then when the two people get married, they discover they have been sold a bill of goods. The marriage isn't what they thought it would be—and one or both parties want out.

It is my contention that one reason so many people are having so much trouble in their marriages today is that they are marrying sociologically instead of theologically. That is, their marriages are based more on social conventions and family expectations than on solid biblical foundations. It's no wonder, then, that many husbands and wives have little idea what they should be doing to make their marriages work.

We are going to address the man's role in this marriage guide, but I also want to note briefly the woman's role because the two are side by side in a crucial passage that closes the Bible's most extensive discussion of the marital relationship. In Ephesians 5:33 we read, "Each individual among you also is to *love* his own wife even as himself, and the wife must see to it that she *respects* her husband" (italics added).

These two highlighted words are a concise summary of the responsibilities that husbands and wives have toward each other. Husbands are commanded to love their wives, and wives are commanded to respect their husbands. Since this marriage guide is dedicated to the man's role in the home, we're going to talk about what it means for a husband to love his wife.

The book of Ephesians 5:25–31 spells out in detail how a husband is to treat his wife. I want to begin with the basic command that encompasses a husband's calling: "Husbands, love your wives, just as Christ also loved the church" (v. 25a).

The word "love" has been tossed around flippantly and reduced to its lowest common denominator today, to the point that many people don't see any difference between the statements "I love yogurt" and "I love my wife."

That's why we need to begin by reminding ourselves that the Bible's definition of love is so much more than personal taste or preference, or even affection. The biblical concept of agape love involves giving of yourself for the benefit of another, even at your own expense. Biblical love is defined by passionately and righteously seeking the well-being of another. Biblical love is an act of the will and not just a fuzzy feeling in the stomach. That's why God can command us to love one another. Love really has nothing to do with whether you feel loving at a particular moment. It has to do with the need of the person being loved, not the feelings of the one doing the loving. We'll see later how this love applies to a marital relationship.

With this definition of love in hand, we are ready to consider three practical ways that a husband can fulfill his role: by becoming his wife's savior, sanctifier, and satisfier.

Becoming Your Wife's Savior

The first way that a man is to love his wife is by becoming her savior. Don't get shook up by that term because we're using it strictly in a nonreligious sense to capture the force of Paul's command that husbands are to love their wives the way Christ loves the church.

That means we need to find out how Christ loves the church because that's the standard we husbands need to attain before we can legitimately be classified as lovers. Every man I know wants to be a lover, so let's find out what it takes to love our wives as Jesus Christ loves His church.

Now before we begin our study, I want to ask you to lay aside what you've heard about love and marriage on the street, on television, or in the movies, and maybe even from your family background, and simply let God's Word speak to you directly.

There are at least three principles or truths that every husband needs to know about loving his wife based on Jesus' love for the church. Even if you're not yet married, I would encourage you to take note of these because they are at the heart of being a successful husband. We can summarize these things in three words: sacrifice, suffering, and substitution.

SACRIFICING FOR YOUR WIFE

How did Christ love the church? First, "[He] gave Himself up for her" (Ephesians 5:25b). That's referring to the sacrifice Jesus made on the cross so that sinners like you and me can be saved. So if a husband's love for his wife is to be like Christ's love for the church, we could say that his love should be cruciform—in the shape of a cross.

Now, most men don't want to hear about crosses and sacrifice. We want to hear about how we're supposed to be wearing a crown as the king of our castle.

Well, I have some news for all of us. Jesus wore a crown, but it was a crown of thorns on his way to the cross. And He's wearing a crown today as King of heaven, but the cross came first. You don't get the crown without the cross. To put it another way, you don't get the glory of Easter without the pain of the cross.

So although most men want to talk about the glory of love, the first thing God wants to know about you as a husband is this: When your wife looks at you, does she see a cross? God wants you to be a look-alike of Jesus, a "little Jesus" in your home by the sacrificial way you love your wife.

We men are great at rapping our love. We can sound very impressive to a woman, talking about how we will be there for her and protect her and even die for her if necessary.

But we're not crazy. We know that the chances of this happening are very remote. I personally can't think of one man I know who has been shot or stabbed or mauled defending his wife from a crazed intruder, and chances are you can't either. That's not going to happen to most of us, or to anyone we know. So we're pretty safe declaring how we would make the ultimate sacrifice for our wife.

But for most of us, it's another story when it comes to the everyday stuff of married life—the sacrificing of our desires, opinions, preferences, and plans for our wives. When God calls husbands to give themselves up for their wives, He is not simply talking about being willing to die. Sacrificing for our wives involves being willing to nail our desires and our agenda to the cross to love our wives and meet their needs.

> GOD WANTS YOU TO BE A LOOK-
> ALIKE OF JESUS, A "LITTLE JESUS" IN
> YOUR HOME BY THE SACRIFICIAL WAY
> YOU LOVE YOUR WIFE.

This brings us to the area where we fail as husbands so often, which is selfishness. Men are often reluctant to give up their wants and their agendas, when necessary, for their wives. Yet a husband should let his wife see that she is of such infinite value in his eyes that he would lay aside anything for her well-being.

The question of a husband's sacrifice is very simple: If I gave your wife a piece of paper and asked her to list what you have given up that's of value to you because of what she needs, desires, or cherishes, how long would her list be?

If I asked her in what ways you have adjusted your plans and schedule in the past month because you saw that she had a burden or a need you could help meet, would she be able to recall such times?

If not, my friend, you have stopped sacrificing. You have stopped representing Jesus in your home.

Now a husband may say his wife didn't remember something, or that there were other circumstances involved. But the point is that our sacrifice should be visible as well as verbal. We need to play as good a game as we talk. In other words, our wives shouldn't have to ransack their memories to try to recall the last time we did something for them that qualified as sacrificial because they benefited from it, even though it cost us.

Let me illustrate what I mean by using Christ's example. Is there anything fuzzy or hard to recall about the reality of His sacrifice for us and how we benefited from it? Of course not. The only reason we are saved is because Jesus went to the cross and laid down His life so we could pass from death to life and move from hell to heaven.

And just in case someone may miss the extent of Jesus Christ's sacrifice, Paul wrote these words:

Although [Jesus] existed in the form of God, [He] did not regard equality with God a thing to be grasped, but emptied Himself, taking the form of a bond-servant, and being made in the likeness of men. Being found in appearance as a man, He humbled Himself by becoming obedient to the point of death, even death on a cross. (Philippians 2:6–8)

Before we sinful human beings came along, Jesus never had to experience hunger or thirst or pain. He was never lonely or mistreated or misunderstood. He wasn't hounded to death before He entered this world and gave His life as a sacrifice for you and me. He left the splendor of heaven for the misery and suffering of earth, all because of His love for us.

Jesus could have adopted the attitude that some husbands have: "I am not about to sacrifice myself for someone who doesn't appreciate my effort and doesn't sacrifice anything for me." Praise God that Jesus didn't take this position, or we would be in big trouble. Jesus gave Himself up for the church.

One of the interesting places where you hear "give yourself up" terminology today is in the game of baseball, which has a play called the sacrifice bunt.

The basic play is simple. The batter gives up his chance to take his three swings at the ball so he can lay down a bunt and move the runner or runners along. The batter who sacrifices is almost always thrown out at first. In fact, that's the plan because he doesn't want the runner or runners ahead of him to be thrown out and lose the chance to score.

What's interesting is the mental process involved

when a batter looks up and sees the third-base coach give the bunt sign. The need for a sacrifice bunt often comes at a crucial point in the game, when one run could make the difference between winning and losing.

In other words, the batter who gets the sacrifice sign is being asked to give up his chance to be "the man," the hero, in a tight situation. He can't flex his muscles and show what he can do with his bat. His job is to tap out a meek bunt and get thrown out at first for the greater good of the team.

I think you know where I'm going with this. God has called every husband to lay down a sacrifice bunt for his wife, so to speak. On a day-to-day basis, this may simply mean not always having to have your way just because you're the leader in the home. Sacrifice involves what is best for the other person, not necessarily what is best for us. Jesus gave up heaven to save us, not because He had to, but because He chose to.

Jesus' sacrifice tells husbands what it means to love. We love by choice, not by feeling. As we said earlier, loving your wife today has little to do with whether you feel like being loving today. Biblical love is generated by the need of the person being loved, not necessarily the feelings or wishes of the one doing the loving.

When the desires of the one who is doing the loving and the needs of the one being loved come together, that's great. The Bible says that Jesus endured the cross "for the joy set before Him" (Hebrews 12:2). His joy was in the knowledge that His sacrifice would purchase our redemption. He was joyful because of His great love for us (see Ephesians 2:4).

That's important because we're not saying that a husband's act of sacrificing for his wife should be a painful thing. He doesn't need to grit his teeth and grunt and do it because he knows it's best for her. When you love your wife the way Christ loves the church, sacrificing for her can bring great delight because you know you have brought joy to her.

But even when sacrifice does hurt and involves real cost to a husband, he is still called to lay aside his wishes for the good of his wife. Too many marriages are hurting because there is no sacrifice involved.

SUFFERING FOR YOUR WIFE

When a man decides to love his wife with Christlike love, then in addition to sacrifice there will be suffering. You can't give up something that is important or valuable to you and not suffer.

When Jesus Christ was in the garden, He prayed, "My Father, if it is possible, let this cup pass from Me" (Matthew 26:39). The cross was traumatic for Jesus to face because He knew it meant such great suffering. His human spirit was engulfed in agony as He looked ahead to the crucifixion.

But Christ also knew there was no other way to accomplish our redemption, so He concluded His prayer by saying, "Yet not as I will, but as You will." Sacrifice brings suffering.

To love your wife with self-sacrificial love is going to hurt sometimes. Jesus called us as His people to take up our cross and follow Him (see Mark 8:34).

> # BIBLICAL LOVE IS GENERATED BY THE NEED OF THE PERSON BEING LOVED, NOT NECESSARILY THE FEELINGS OR WISHES OF THE ONE DOING THE LOVING.

You didn't think the cross was only for Christ, did you? My favorite verse in the Bible tells us otherwise. It is a verse that I say every morning to myself when I wake up and start my day. Galatians 2:20 says, "I have been crucified with Christ; and it is no longer I who live, but Christ lives in me; and the life which I now live in the flesh I live by faith in the Son of God, who loved me and gave Himself up for me."

We also must die to ourselves daily to follow Christ, and for husbands this includes dying to our plans and our preferences in order to love our wives as ourselves. Nailing these things to the cross can hurt. But again, you can't get to the glory of Easter and the resurrection without enduring the cross and dying to yourself.

Besides surrendering your own desires and plans, let me mention another way that showing Christ's love to your wife may hurt. It may hurt because she may not respond immediately in the way you would like her to respond. She may doubt your sincerity or turn a cold shoulder to your attempts at sacrificial love.

I say that because what we're talking about here is not a magic wand a husband can wave over his marriage and instantly erase years of frustration or hurt. A husband may have to persevere through a period of mistrust, skepticism, or even hostility in order to break through the protective shell that his wife has built up around her heart.

That's why a husband needs to take his cue from Christ and hang in there. By that I mean a husband needs to keep on loving his wife regardless of whether she appreciates or even deserves his sacrifice.

This is the way Christ loved us. Paul said in Romans 5 that it's easy to love people when they're good and nice. "But God demonstrates His own love toward us, in that while we were yet sinners, Christ died for us" (Romans 5:8). We weren't nice, and we weren't easy to love. But Jesus didn't say that if we would treat Him right, He would love us. He loved us even when we were ignoring Him and trampling His love in the dirt.

I hope you know that Jesus could have come down from the cross. As the old gospel song says, "He could have called ten thousand angels." Jesus didn't have to stay on the cross, but love nailed Him there.

Jesus was willing to suffer and die for us, and God is asking husbands to imitate His Son in their homes. But that's hard for men to do because by nature we are deal-makers. Many husbands make deals with their wives, even if they never actually verbalize it. "If you meet my sexual needs, I'll love you. If you cook my food and let me watch sports and don't spend too much money, everything will be fine."

But when we start putting conditions on our love, we have redefined love and taken it away from the biblical meaning. Again, I'm not saying it will always be easy, because you may not get the response you were looking for.

One man told me, "My wife is keeping me from loving her!" I know what he meant, because his marriage was in rough shape. But I still had to point out to him that he was starting in the wrong place. Christlike love doesn't make "if you will, I will" deals.

You may say, "Tony, this kind of love sounds pretty risky. You're saying I may have to risk misunderstanding, mistreatment, or even rejection in order to love and serve my wife. You're saying I have to risk crucifixion!"

That's right. The love I'm talking about is risky, and it involves a cross. That's why your faith has to be not in your ability to love, or even in the response of your wife, but in the God "who raises the dead" (2 Corinthians 1:9).

Jesus knew that if He went all the way to Calvary to bleed and die for our sins, His Father would raise Him from the dead. You say, "But God isn't raising me from the grave. I'm not experiencing His resurrection power in my marriage."

Maybe it's because you haven't died to yourself yet. You can't resurrect folk who aren't dead. True love involves suffering, even to the point of going to the cross.

SUBSTITUTING FOR YOUR WIFE

The third way that a husband shows Christlike love to his wife is by substitution.

We read about Jesus' substitutionary death for us in Romans 5:8. He took our place and took the stroke for our sin. We were the ones who deserved to be on the cross. There was no question about who was right and who was wrong when it came to Jesus becoming our substitute. We had no argument to offer Him to justify ourselves.

> MEN, IF YOU WANT TO SEE YOUR
> WIFE BLOSSOM INTO A LOVING,
> RESPONSIVE MATE, THE MARITAL
> BALL IS IN YOUR COURT.

So if a husband is going to be a savior, a Christlike example in his home, he must be willing to bear the stroke without fighting over who is right or fighting for his right to be right and have the last word.

Men are detectives at heart. Maybe it comes from watching too many old "whodunit" movies. But we like to get in there and figure out who said what first and who did what. We like to sift through all the evidence so we can track down the culprit and make sure justice is done and the guilty party is fingered.

Of course, our wives usually approach marital conflict or disagreement from a totally different perspective. They're more interested in the personal and emotional implications of the conflict than in arguing about who started it or who's right.

This means there will be occasions when a husband may feel justified in insisting that he is right. But the emotional fallout from taking that position far outweighs the momentary satisfaction of saying, "I'm right, and you know it." There's such a thing as winning the momentary battle and losing the marital war.

This thing of being right and justifying ourselves is a big one for men. We're wired in such a way that we like to be right, and we like for other people to know that we are right—even when we are wrong! We'll even lie sometimes rather than admit that we don't know what we're talking about.

One of the more common areas where this tendency shows up is in driving. There isn't a man alive who doesn't believe deep down that he could follow a trail through trackless woods like Daniel Boone. Now I can assure you that Daniel Boone's wife never said to him, "Honey, are you sure you know where you're going?" But our wives often ask us that question. And we can be sweating bullets, looking desperately for a road sign or an exit. But we're not going to admit we're lost. "Oh yeah, I know exactly where we are."

Women don't understand that to ask us to pull off and ask for help stings our manhood. So we keep plowing ahead, praying under our breath, "Father, show me which way to go."

I have this same problem, compounded by the fact that I hate to stop for gas. I know how far our car can go once the gas gauge hits the "E," so I'm not afraid to pass up a few gas stations.

This drives my wife to distraction, and it almost cost me big time once when I kept passing stations on the freeway and she kept gently suggesting that I might want to stop at the next station. I kept going, and sure enough by the time I really needed gas and started sweating, I couldn't find a station.

I could see my whole marital life flashing before my eyes as I took an exit in desperation while the car started sputtering. To my great relief, I discovered that the exit was downhill and there was a gas station at the bottom! I coasted up to the pump like nothing was wrong at all.

Men want to be right, but substitution says being right isn't the issue. In fact, let me tell you how wrong you and I were before Jesus Christ. He took our place and bore the punishment for us even when we were at our most vile in terms of being sinners.

After what Jesus has done for you and me, there is nothing that our wives could ever do or say to us that should cause us to refuse to be their substitute. God has commanded us to love our wives even when they don't deserve it—for if we love them only when they deserve it, where would grace be? In fact, we need to love our wives the most when they deserve it the least.

When I counsel a couple who are engaged to be married, we will discuss different areas of their histories that they are bringing into the marriage. One area I ask about is if the bride-to-be has any debt. If she does, then I ask her future husband if he is willing to assume the responsibility for that debt.

He needs to not only acknowledge her debt—and even the poor choices she might have made in accruing it—but he also must assume ownership for her debt if he is going to satisfy his role as husband.

In marriage, if a wife does something that is wrong that brings about negative consequences as a result, a husband should not only seek to forgive his wife, but also to cover her through taking ownership of the consequences. In doing this, he serves as her substitute.

Now before you toss this marriage guide aside because all of this sounds like too much work and too much sacrifice, let me remind you of something. Women are responders. They are wired to respond positively to love, attention, and caring.

I asked a question of the married women in our

church in Dallas: "If your husband lavished on you the kind of sacrificial, suffering, substitutionary love that Jesus Christ lavishes on the church, would you have any good news for him?" The response was overwhelmingly positive. I'm convinced this is what our wives are longing for—and starving for, in some cases—even if they don't state it in theological terms.

Men, if you want to see your wife blossom into a loving, responsive mate, the marital ball is in your court.

2

THE ROLE
OF SANCTIFIER

BECOMING YOUR WIFE'S SANCTIFIER

We just looked at several ways a man can fulfill his role as savior in his wife's life and now we want to look at another way that a man can fulfill His God-given role in his home. The Bible says that just as Christ is the Sanctifier of the church, so a husband is to be his wife's sanctifier.

Our text for this section is Ephesians 5:26–27. We need to repeat verse 25 for context, since verse 26 is the continuation of the sentence: "Husbands, love your wives, just as Christ also loved the church and gave Himself up for her, so that He might sanctify her, having cleansed her by the washing of water with the word, that He might present to Himself the church in all her glory, having no spot or wrinkle or any such thing; but that she would be holy and blameless."

To sanctify someone or something means to set it apart from common or ordinary usage for a special purpose—to make it holy. In the Bible, people or things were set apart for God's use. They may have been common objects or ordinary people, but once they were sanctified they became very special.

Sometimes people in our church ask me to dedicate their house to God's glory. Many people also dedicate their infant children to the Lord. These are examples of sanctification.

When a person is sanctified, he is set apart from his past unto his future. This has application to marriage because when a man marries a woman, he sets her apart from her past and unto a future that he has promised to her.

Most new husbands make glorious promises about the future, and those promises don't always come to fruition. But the point is that there is a setting apart, a disconnection from the past and a new connection with the future.

You see, a great disconnection occurs in a marriage. The husband and wife are disconnected from previous relationships, and the only reason a woman should make that switch is that her future with her husband looks better than her past with her parents because he is sanctifying her, or setting her apart, as unique and special.

Sanctification is a glorious term that describes the process of our Christian growth from the moment we were saved until we enter heaven. To borrow from the analogy of marriage, Jesus Christ did not simply say "I do" as your Savior and then leave you standing at the altar. He committed Himself to be with you as your Sanctifier from that moment on to bring you from where you are to where He wants you to be.

Christ is doing this today with each believer who collectively makes up the church. The church is His bride, and He is preparing her for the marriage supper of the Lamb so that she might appear on her wedding day in all of her radiance.

> ## TO SANCTIFY SOMEONE OR SOMETHING MEANS TO SET IT APART FROM COMMON OR ORDINARY USAGE FOR A SPECIAL PURPOSE—TO MAKE IT HOLY.

This is a picture of what a husband should be doing for his wife on an ongoing basis. This has to do with the quality of his spiritual leadership in the home, which we are going to discuss in detail.

By the way, before we move on please note that both Christian husbands and wives can have a godly influence in their homes (see 1 Corinthians 7:14). An unbelieving partner in a marriage is "sanctified" or set apart by the sanctifying presence of the believing partner, and their children are also "holy" in the sense of being set apart by the blessings that accrue to such a home.

But Ephesians 5:26–27 also makes it clear that the husband is uniquely called to be the sanctifier in his home. So before you think about departing a troubled marriage, men, think about the impact on your family.

The last verse of the Old Testament ends with a curse on a land in which fathers are alienated from their children—which is the curse of our culture. We have a generation of children with no fathers living at home, and so they are going off in all kinds of wrong directions. Why? Because they are no longer being sanctified by the presence of a godly father.

THE REQUIREMENT FOR SANCTIFICATION

A husband who wants to be his wife's sanctifier must first become her savior. That's the pattern Christ established.

Since we have dealt with this, let me just mention again that the role of a savior involves death. So if your wife isn't responding to you and encouraging you and following your leadership in the home, maybe it's because you haven't been to the cross for her yet.

The goal of sanctification is to change us from something we are into something we ought to be, so that we think differently, act differently, walk differently, talk differently, behave differently, and react differently. For the Christian this process of transformation must begin with a death, because God is not going to mess around trying to fix up and patch up our old sinful nature. We must die to ourselves and live to God.

So it is with marriage. A husband is called to die to his own plans and desires so he can serve and love his wife. And in the process, he becomes qualified to be his wife's sanctifier. Until you are ready to die to yourself, don't expect your efforts to bring about real change in your wife.

THE PROCESS OF SANCTIFICATION

This is where I want to spend some serious time because it is so crucial that you understand how sanctification in marriage works. A lot of husbands wish their wives would change in a certain area, whether it's in how they communicate, the way they deal with family members, or any number of things. It's important to realize that sanctification says something does need to change.

When we come to Christ we are saved in a moment, but most of us have habits, attitudes, and other baggage we bring into our Christian lives that Christ needs to deal with. So we ought to be concerned about how we and other Christians are doing in becoming more like Jesus Christ. Salvation is instantaneous; sanctification is a lifelong process that involves replacing the distortion in our souls with the truth of the Word of God as well as allowing this truth to dominate our lives through the growth of our spirit.

According to our text in Ephesians 5:26, Jesus cleanses the church "by the washing of water with the word." One of my roles as a pastor is to minister the Word of God to the church as a representative of Jesus Christ.

Guess what this means for a husband's calling in his marriage? I know this is not what most men want to hear, but what the Bible is saying is that a husband is to function as his wife's pastor. Just as God has called me to be pastor over His house at our church in Dallas, so you, if you are a Christian husband, are to be pastor over your house.

Now I can almost hear the groans, because it has been my experience that far too many husbands are not fulfilling the pastoral role in their homes. (Sometimes this ministry is referred to as a man being the priest in his home in terms of leading his family before God. I prefer the term "pastor," for reasons that will be clear as we go along.)

Someone may say, "Come on, Tony, I'm not trained to do that pastor stuff. That's why we have preachers like you." Well, I'll show you later why this kind of thinking has holes in it. A husband who wants to take seriously his leadership and spiritual responsibility in marriage, and help his wife blossom into all that God intended her to be, must be ready to shepherd her the way a pastor shepherds his flock. Women are wired to respond to loving leadership.

Let me explain why your wife needs you to be her

sanctifier, beyond the fact that all of us need to grow and mature in Christ. When you married your wife, you also married her history—that is, everything that made her who she was up to the time that you met her and became part of her life.

All of us tend to hide some of this stuff when we're dating. We want to put our best foot forward and make a good impression. It's impossible for any two people to know everything that can be known about each other's families and backgrounds before they marry. Or if we see something that troubles us, we figure we can change it once we're married.

So there are always surprises because all of our souls have been distorted either through our own sin or someone else's sin and its effect on us as we grew up. Because our soul makes up the part of us that contains our mind, will, and emotions, we don't always behave or respond to things in life as we should. We also often carry around wrong attitudes, opinions, and ideas that lead to messed-up relationships that tend to come to the surface as a marriage progresses.

The same thing happens in the church. When I meet people for the first time in our membership class, they all look holy. But then as we get to know each other, often things come out that prove the truth that all of us are dragging around remnants of a distorted view of life through a tainted soul.

The purpose of the church is to minister the Word of God to its people in such a way that the Word does its work of pruning and convicting and shaping them into the image of Christ. As the Word goes out and is received and allowed to abide deeply within our soul, thus causing our spirit to begin to grow and dominate our mind, will, and emotions, change happens because Jesus is washing His bride the church with the water of the Word. What Jesus does for His bride, a husband is to do for his bride. He is to become her pastor.

WOMEN ARE WIRED TO RESPOND TO LOVING LEADERSHIP.

There are plenty of men who want to be the head of their homes and want their wives and children to know they are in charge. But when it comes to being the pastor in their home, too many Christian husbands are missing in action.

I doubt if our church would like it if the pastor was absent two out of every three Sundays when they came to church to feed on God's Word and worship God. People wouldn't take it too well if the pastor was never there when they had a need.

I'm going to be at church to minister to God's people because that's my commitment and my responsibility. It's also my joy and delight, and that's the way God wants husbands to feel about their ministry to their wives. Don't go around proclaiming, "I am the head of this house," if you are not also willing to say to your wife and children, "I am also the pastor of this house, and I intend to fulfill my calling."

The Bible is so serious about a husband's pastoral role that Paul told the Corinthians, "The women are to keep silent in the churches; for they are not permitted to speak, but are to subject themselves, just as the Law also says. If they desire to learn anything, let them ask their own husbands at home; for it is improper for a woman to speak in church" (1 Corinthians 14:34–35).

This chapter deals with the importance of maintaining proper order in the church assembly as opposed to the disorder and chaos that marked the church at Corinth. Notice that one of the solutions to this problem is for husbands to exercise their pastoral role at home by ministering to their wives.

So when a woman has questions or wants to know something, the first pastor she should turn to is not the pastor in the pulpit, but the pastor shepherding her own home. She should have her private pastor she can go to any time, a shepherd who knows how to open up the Word and minister to his family. Men, you are the pastor of your home.

I mentioned above the objection that many men would raise, which is that they are not trained for this job. Paul was not saying that a husband needs to know the answer to every Bible question or be able to explain every passage. But he should be growing in his knowledge of the Word to the point that he can open the Bible at home and guide his wife and family.

This means the husband also needs a teacher, which is the task of the church. I told the men in our church that we are going to be there every week to teach the Word but that they also have a responsibility to be there ready to learn.

It may sound like I'm describing an ideal situation in which godly men are learning and growing in the Word and teaching their families. But that's exactly the point. This is not meant to be the ideal, but the norm, in the body of Christ.

As Christian men we have to get away from this mentality that we take our Bible to church on Sunday, listen to the sermon, then go home and put the Bible back wherever it goes until the next week.

I had to go to class every week in seminary and put forth a lot of work to learn the Bible so I would have something to say when I came to the house of God. Spiritual headship in the church and the home is a calling that demands our best effort and attention.

So let me ask you some questions. How many times a week do you have devotions and pray with your wife? Do you know the needs and burdens that are uppermost on her heart right now because the two of you are regularly bringing them to the Lord? Can you open the Word and apply its truth to the situations your family faces? If your wife were to need guidance or spiritual insight, would she have to skip over you and go outside the home to find someone in tune with God?

I know these are convicting questions, but they're unavoidable because we are talking about what it means to be a pastor. Don't expect your congregation at home to get with the program if you as the pastor hardly ever show up in the pulpit.

So I need to ask you, Have you become the pastor in your home yet? If your wife has to go to church to find a pastor, then you are giving another man more influence over your wife and family than you have. Now don't misunderstand. It's important to have a pastor at church. But while your wife may receive pastoring twice a week at church, she ought to be in your church every day, being shepherded by her pastor at home.

Let me remind you that we're talking about sanctification, the process of becoming less and less like our old selves and becoming more and more like Jesus Christ. The way this happens is by our growth in grace through the cleansing of the Word as we apply God's truth to our lives.

This growth certainly involves pointing out what is wrong that needs to be fixed, but it doesn't stop there. I say that because men are notorious for being critics. In the context of marriage, we can see what's wrong with our wives, where their flaws are, and what we don't like, and we're often quick to point out the problems.

But even if those observations are valid, they're not enough by themselves. Your wife needs a coach, not a critic. Sports commentators are good at analyzing a play from up in the booth and telling the fans why it didn't work. But the team needs a coach who shows up at practice every day and says, "Let me show you why that play went wrong and how to fix it."

In other words, criticizing is not the same as exercising pastoral care. You've heard the old line, "Everybody's a critic." There's a lot of truth to that because it's much easier to see what's wrong in others than it is to come alongside them and offer help toward a solution.

IF YOUR WIFE WERE TO NEED GUIDANCE OR SPIRITUAL INSIGHT, WOULD SHE HAVE TO SKIP OVER YOU AND GO OUTSIDE THE HOME TO FIND SOMEONE IN TUNE WITH GOD?

One thing that will help you function as the pastor in your home is to think about what does and does not help you to grow and learn as a Christian. I'm guessing that like most people, you do a lot better under patient, constructive teaching than under harsh criticism that only points out what is wrong.

So if you need someone to give you time, patience, and teaching to grow, you should be willing to extend that same grace to your wife. A pastor can't skip over problems, but he should also be a person who gives hope. And hope is always there, because God will never give up on His children. He has promised to finish His "good work" in us (Philippians 1:6).

It has been well said that a shepherd *leads* his sheep; he doesn't drive them. But leading means that you're out front, showing the way and saying, in effect, "Imitate me."

Now this is where it gets sticky for many husbands. The reason they can't pastor their wives is that they aren't growing and maturing themselves. Jesus didn't have this problem because He is the sinless Son of God who gave Himself for the church. But as sinners saved by grace, husbands need to heed the Bible's admonition to "grow in the grace and knowledge of our Lord and Savior Jesus Christ" (2 Peter 3:18). Earlier in his letter to the Ephesians, Paul had written, "I . . . implore you to walk in a manner worthy of the calling with which you have been called" (4:1).

A husband who is stagnant spiritually is in no position to lead his wife. As I say in the companion guide to this booklet, *For Married Women Only*, it's hard to follow a parked car.

Jesus is cleansing His bride, and a husband is responsible for the cleansing of his bride. By that I mean he should be leading her into a deeper and holier relationship with Christ. But he can only do that as he is allowing the Word of God to change and mold him into the image of Christ.

What about the husband who says, "But my wife doesn't really want to grow spiritually"? Then you continue to love her and provide the example of Christ in your home that will draw her to Him and to you.

Another husband may say, "But my wife is working against me right now. I feel like I married the enemy." Well, Jesus commanded us to love our enemies. A husband who is in a difficult situation still has the obligation to be the lover and leader of his wife.

Sanctification is a process that won't ever be complete this side of heaven, which means there is always room for growth and always hope that a person can change. Instead of looking for miracles or quick fixes, husbands are called to show consistent love and biblical leadership that helps their wives grow into the full radiance of the inner and outer beauty that God designed them to have.

THE RESULTS OF SANCTIFICATION

What can a husband expect if he takes on the job of being his wife's sanctifier, the job of being pastor in his home?

What he can expect is a transformed bride. The Bible says Jesus is sanctifying His church "that He might present to Himself the church in all her glory, having no spot or wrinkle or any such thing; but that she would be holy and blameless" (Ephesians 5:27).

How many husbands in their right minds would not want to see their wives transformed into brides of spotless glory and beauty? That's where her sanctification is designed to lead.

Now you may think this is something beyond your capability as a husband to pull off. Let me remind you first that you aren't doing it yourself. The Holy Spirit is at work in you and in your wife to bring about spiritual growth and maturity, so don't ever think you have to do this yourself.

But having said that, my contention is that most men don't understand the extent of the authority God has given them in their marriages and their homes. To explain what I mean, we need to go back to Adam.

God gave Adam the job of naming all the animals, according to Genesis 2:19–20. Adam could give any animal any name he wanted. Now you need to understand that in the Bible, to name something is to have authority over it. God had told mankind to subdue and rule over the earth and the animals (see Genesis 1:28). One way Adam exercised that authority was by naming the animals.

But then God fashioned Eve and brought her to Adam (see Genesis 2:22). Adam had never seen a creature like this before. What was he going to do? The first thing he did was name this lovely creation standing before him, which he realized was taken from his own flesh and corresponded to him. "She shall be called Woman, because she was taken out of Man" (v. 23).

The Hebrew words here are interesting because the word for man is 'ish and the word for woman is 'isha, which means "taken from man." So what Adam did was give Eve his name.

This is the origin of the practice of a wife taking her husband's name. That is far more than a legal move or a convenience in identifying a married couple. It is a statement of God's original intent in marriage, and really the first act of submission that a wife performs for her husband. That's why the practice has fallen into such disfavor with so many women who insist on going into marriage on a fifty-fifty basis.

But the reason God brought Eve to Adam to be named is that He intended the man to take dominion in the home—not as a king wielding his scepter and lording it over his subjects, but as a loving spiritual leader whose purpose is to sanctify his bride. Out of that dominion in the home would flow a greater capacity to exercise dominion in his sphere of influence. In fact, the marriage covenant was established, as we see in the book of Genesis, in order to enable couples to carry out their divinely given right to rule their world, within the boundaries of God's sovereignty.

I go into much greater detail about this topic in the companion guide on marriage covenant, *Marriage Matters*, and I would encourage you to pick up a copy of this guide because it is a powerful tool to use in transforming the way you view your marriage.

That's why I said earlier that a wife should be able to go into marriage with the promise and the prospect that her future with her husband is going to be more glorious than her past with her parents. Because when she unites with her husband in this new relationship, she is also given the ability to rule her world at a level that she never had when she was on her own.

Through a proper understanding and application of the covenant of marriage, a husband who seeks to follow God should be able to promise his wife a growing, sanctifying relationship. Not perfect bliss or utopia, but movement in the right direction.

You see, we as believers can never say that we are worse off now than we were the day Jesus found us. When Christ found you and me, we were deep in sin. Like the prodigal son, we were caked with dirt from the pigpen, and we smelled awful in the nostrils of God.

But Jesus didn't leave us in the pigpen. He got dirty with the mud and the pain of this world to bring us out of that mess, clean us up, dress us in white robes as His bride, and set in motion a lifetime process of making us glorious and radiant.

What Jesus does for the church, a man is to do for his wife. And when the process starts to work, something wonderful happens. The bride is described as "having no spot or wrinkle" (Ephesians 5:27).

Now every woman knows about spots and wrinkles. A spot is a defilement on the outside, while a wrinkle is in the very fabric. But while spots and wrinkles may be inevitable in the physical realm with age, spiritually, a woman should be growing into a being of such beauty that these signs of deterioration and defilement are fading away.

The Bible says that although our outer person is "decaying," our inner person "is being renewed day by day"

(2 Corinthians 4:16). That's a wonderful summary of what it means to be sanctified, transformed into the image of Jesus Christ.

> THE MARRIAGE COVENANT WAS
> ESTABLISHED, AS WE SEE IN THE
> BOOK OF GENESIS, IN ORDER TO
> ENABLE COUPLES TO CARRY OUT
> THEIR DIVINELY GIVEN RIGHT
> TO RULE THEIR WORLD.

If we could bottle a formula that would make spots and wrinkles disappear, we would be besieged by people clamoring for it. No such product exists, but this is what Jesus offers to those of us who belong to His church. And a husband can enhance this process for his wife by helping her grow in spiritual beauty and glory until she is transformed before his eyes.

But to do that, he has to get dirty by dealing with the stuff in his own life and in his wife's life that defiles and needs to go. Jesus got bloody dealing with sin, but His blood was necessary to cleanse sin. A clean heart and life is the result every husband should seek for himself and his wife.

3

THE ROLE
OF SATISFIER

BECOMING YOUR WIFE'S SATISFIER

We're now ready for the third and final portion of this study on a man's role in the home. A man who is committed to being his wife's savior and sanctifier will also have a desire to satisfy her deepest needs.

Paul continued his instruction to husbands by saying, "So husbands ought also to love their own wives as their own bodies. He who loves his own wife loves himself" (Ephesians 5:28). Unless we're talking about a case where a wife is deliberately trying to undermine her husband, when you look at a man's wife, you should get a pretty good idea of what he thinks about himself.

If a wife is miserable all the time, maybe it's because she is married to a miserable man. If her countenance is bright, chances are she is being nourished and cherished by a loving husband. Our wives are like mirrors, reflecting back to us what kinds of husbands we are.

MEETING YOUR WIFE'S NEEDS

The Bible makes it clear that satisfying your wife involves meeting her needs. Remember that the example for a husband is Jesus' love and care for the church. Jesus has taken it upon Himself, as Husband of His bride, to meet her every need.

Most of us men talk a better game when we're dating than we actually play after we're married. We can rap all day about how we are going to be there for our lady and take care of all her needs.

Now I know what you're saying. "But I didn't know my wife was that needy." Well, that just means you have to work a little harder. Don't you think the church, the bride of Christ, was needy when He met us? We were covered in our sin and filth, but Jesus gave Himself to clean us up and make us radiant.

Jesus committed Himself to meet the church's needs because He understands something about leadership that most men don't, which is that the higher you go, the greater the servant you become. Men often define leadership in terms of being the boss. "I'm in charge here. This is my home. I am the king of this castle."

That's the attitude Jesus' disciples had as they reclined with Him at the Last Supper the night He was betrayed.

They got into a dispute about who was the greatest (see Luke 22:24). So Jesus said to them, "The one who is the greatest among you must become like the youngest, and the leader like the servant" (v. 26).

Jesus also demonstrated what He meant when He got up from the table, wrapped a towel around His waist, and washed the disciples' feet (see John 13:3–5). Somebody else should have performed that act of service for the group, but the disciples were too busy trying to figure out who was the greatest. Nobody wanted to take the role of a servant.

When He was finished, Jesus sat down and taught the principle of servant leadership. "You call me Teacher and Lord; and you are right, for so I am. If I then, the Lord and the Teacher, washed your feet, you also ought to wash one another's feet. For I gave you an example that you also should do as I did to you" (vv. 13–15).

Since this is how Jesus meets the needs of the church, we husbands must do the same for our wives. We must take the initiative and set the pace in our homes by serving our wives instead of sitting around waiting for them to serve us.

God's love, which is doing what's best for the other person regardless of the cost to you, certainly includes being a servant. A servant serves whether he feels like it or not because that's his calling.

Now you may be saying, "Doesn't the Bible say something about a wife calling her husband lord?" Yes, in 1 Peter 3:1–6 the apostle described the way a wife is to honor and reverence her husband, using Sarah's example as she called Abraham "lord" (v. 6). We're going to look at this passage later because it ends with a word to husbands. But here suffice it to say that you will make it far more conducive for your wife to honor you if you are committed to serving her.

If you want to obey the Lord by loving your wife as your own body, here's a simple principle: Whatever you do to pamper and care for yourself, make sure you double it for your wife because she is an extension of you.

Here's a very practical illustration of what I'm talking about. You're sitting on the couch watching a football game when hunger pangs strike. You're dying for something to eat, but emotionally you don't feel like getting up because you're tired and comfortable and the game is in progress.

But when the hunger pangs start knocking you around until you can't take it anymore, you will get up and make your way to the refrigerator. Why? Because meeting your need is more important than your emotional feeling of not wanting to move. If you'll do that to care for your own body, why wouldn't you do the same to meet your wife's needs?

I know some husbands are afraid that if they start doing this, their wives are going to take advantage of them. Well, let me make two observations. First, many wives have the same fear concerning their duty to submit to their husbands. So if you're feeling this way, you're not alone. Second, that's a risk you'll have to take. Look at

Jesus. He took the greatest risk of all to love us, and we have all abused His love. But He continues to love us because His love had nothing to do with our worthiness and everything to do with His promise to seek our best. There is a risk involved in making it your goal to meet the needs of another person. But true, godly love takes that risk.

> WE MUST TAKE THE INITIATIVE
> AND SET THE PACE IN OUR HOMES
> BY SERVING OUR WIVES INSTEAD
> OF SITTING AROUND WAITING
> FOR THEM TO SERVE US.

STUDYING AND SERVING YOUR WIFE

In order for you to meet your wife's needs, you have to know what those needs are. That's why Peter said, "You husbands in the same way, live with your wives in an understanding way, as with someone weaker, since she is a woman; and show her honor as a fellow heir of the grace of life, so that your prayers will not be hindered" (1 Peter 3:7).

We husbands are told to study our wives. The reason is that a woman can be difficult to interpret. To begin making a serious effort to understand a woman is to visit a foreign country for most of us men. That's because she's speaking a foreign language, the language of how she feels, and we're speaking the language of instruction, what she should do.

Often a wife sits down to tell her husband something, and after five minutes he's coming up with solutions to a problem she has not yet fully explained. The reason the husband proposes a quick solution is that he doesn't want to take the time to hear his wife's explanation.

See, in your mind it's going to take her two hours to explain something that you think should take about five minutes. What you want her to do is cut off an hour-and-fifty-five minutes' worth of conversation and get to the point because you already have the answer.

The message that many of us communicate to our wives by our demeanor, if not by our words, is, "Look, this is where you're going, this is what you mean, and here's the solution. So we don't have to spend two hours discussing it."

But that's not the point. Your wife doesn't want you to understand the problem intellectually. She wants you to feel it with her, to see how it is affecting her. She wants you to focus in on her and show that you are really listening to what she's saying.

That's part of what it means to live with your wife in an understanding way. It means being there long enough to understand what she is saying and what she means by what she is saying.

That's why when you start trying to fix the problem after five minutes, your wife gets upset with you. She wants to know that you are more concerned about her than her problem. For her, part of the "fix" is having the time she needs to express herself fully and unveil how she feels.

My sermons average about fifty minutes in length, but it takes me twelve hours in the study with the Bible and the books to produce a fifty-minute message. It's the time spent in preparation behind the scenes that validates what happens up front on Sunday or Wednesday.

We as men often want credit for what we do up front in our marriages. But it's the work behind the scenes—the listening and caring, the "dwelling time" we spend seeking to understand our wives—that really tells the story of how we're doing as husbands. That takes time and a servant's heart.

You say, "Yeah, but I don't have time to do all of that." No, you have the time, and so do I. All you have to do is look at how worn the TV remote is to know that you have time. We used to give our wives all the time we had when we were dating them and trying to win them, but now we can't seem to find the time for them.

That doesn't wash, and our wives know it. Have you ever gone to a restaurant and been seated by a server who expressed great joy at your coming, and then disappeared once the meal arrived? As you sit there with your throats parched trying to find your server or get someone's attention, chances are you will not be in the mood to say "thank you" by leaving a big tip when the meal is over.

Let me tell you something. A lot of husbands want a big tip in bed at night. But their wives can't find them or get their attention the rest of the time, so it's no wonder they are frustrated with their husbands' expectations.

How do you know if you're getting the job done when it comes to understanding your wife and serving her? One simple way is to ask her how you're doing—and listen to the answer!

But if that's too threatening, take a piece of paper and draw a line down the middle. On one side list all the ways your wife serves you, and then on the other side list all the ways you serve her. If her list is longer than yours, then you may need to ask yourself if you are fulfilling Jesus' word that the one who wants to be the greatest should be the greatest servant. Your wife should not be outserving you.

NOURISHING AND CHERISHING YOUR WIFE

We're learning that when it comes to the ways a husband needs to care for his wife, the Bible is rich with instruction. That includes Ephesians 5:29, where we are told, "No one ever hated his own flesh, but nourishes and cherishes it, just as Christ also does the church."

The word "nourish" means "to feed in order to mature." Jesus provides all that we need at salvation so we can feed on Him and grow into mature disciples. When we got saved, Jesus didn't stop feeding us. That's when He started.

This is why we should marry in order to date instead of the other way around. Our culture has it backward, especially we men. We nourish and cherish that special person, we lavish her with love and attention, and we bend over backward to serve her, as long as we're trying to win her. But once we're married we stop doing all of that because we figure the chase is over and we won the prize.

But marriage is when the nourishing and cherishing should begin for real, not end. Your wife should be blossoming under your care. She should be better off now than she was when you married her because you are investing so much to help her grow into her full potential as a person.

That doesn't happen all at once. To nourish someone suggests an ongoing process. You have to eat the right things every day in order to grow, not just once a month or whenever you feel like it. Nourishing involves continuing to do the things that made your relationship with your wife blossom in the first place. Briefly, here are five ways a husband can nourish his wife.*

1. *Words of affirmation*. A husband should be his wife's biggest cheerleader. A lot of wives would settle for a "Thank you for dinner" for starters. But we can do better than that. You shouldn't have to look very far to find things your wife is doing right that you can affirm.

* Borrowed from *The Five Love Languages: The Secret to Love that Lasts* (Northfield Publishing, 2010), by Dr. Gary Chapman.

A husband may say, "I'm not very good at that." You must have been pretty good at it when you were dating! Maybe you've just quit trying. We're not necessarily talking about a Shakespearean sonnet, just some thoughtful and well-chosen words that communicate love and value to your wife.

2. *Quality time.* It takes time to nourish your body, and the same is true of your marriage. "Quality time" can be a misnomer for some people who take it to mean giving someone the best five minutes of their day.

   But the only time investment that qualifies as "quality" is a substantial investment in the life of another person who has priority in your life. Now don't go out today and tell your wife that you are going to invest in time with her so you can listen to her, understand her, and talk with her. The shock might be too great for her system. Just start doing it and she'll get the message that she really matters to you.

3. *Giving gifts.* Taking the time to bring your wife a gift, even a small one, is another important way of telling her how much she means to you. Even more than the value of the gift is the idea that she was on your mind and that you had to get her something that says, "Just because I love you."

4. *Acts of service.* We've already talked about the importance of serving our wives. This may involve doing the unexpected, like taking on a job that your wife normally does as a way of expressing your love. You could make the bed, which only takes a few minutes, or stop and fold some clothes the next time you pass by the laundry basket.

> # NOURISHING INVOLVES CONTINUING TO DO THE THINGS THAT MADE YOUR RELATIONSHIP WITH YOUR WIFE BLOSSOM IN THE FIRST PLACE.

5. *Physical touch.* This is nonsexual touch that simply says, "I want to be close to you. I want to hold your hand and put my arm around you." This is another element of nourishing that too often falls by the wayside as the years go by.

The Bible says that a husband who loves his wife as Christ loves the church also "cherishes" her (Ephesians 5:29). The word "cherish" means "to heat up or warm," and it was used of a bird that would spread her feathers over her young. The picture here is one of special care and protection because the person being cared for is of unique and incredible value. A husband cherishes his wife when he treats her as special.

One reason we need to cherish our wives is that according to 1 Peter 3:7, a woman is weaker than a man. Now you probably know that the reference there is to physical strength, not to intellectual ability, moral strength, or any other criterion of personal value. We could liken a husband's treatment of his wife to the way a person treats fine china. You don't handle fine china the way you would handle paper plates, because china breaks easily. You handle china carefully because it carries great value.

Men often want to change their wives, and they often set about it in a harsh, demanding way. But you are not a drill sergeant, your wife is not your new recruit, and marriage is not army boot camp. Most wives are not going to work on problem areas simply because their husbands issue the command, "Change, woman."

When we talked earlier about a husband being his wife's sanctifier, we said that when a man marries a woman he also inherits her history and family and all that made her who she is. This is where a husband's nourishing and cherishing is really important and really needed.

Some women have rough spots because their family made things hard. Maybe a wife had a domineering mother and an absent father, and it's hard for her to trust a man because all she has seen and heard is how men are no good and will let her down.

Whatever the problem or rough spot is, it's your job

as the husband to soften it. Now, if you've ever tried to get hard, baked-on food off a dish, you know you can start scrubbing and rubbing hard, or you can soak that thing in nice, hot, soapy water until the hard stuff is soft.

If you've tried the hard scrubbing in your marriage, you know that this usually winds up with everyone being frustrated. But when you apply the soft soaking of loving care, the change becomes easier and more natural because the methodology is biblical and not secular. Remember, God has created women to be responsive to care. All it takes is the right environment.

We're finally ready for verses 30–31 of Ephesians 5, which is where I want to conclude our study because verses 32–33 are a recap of the principles we've been studying. Paul said that husbands should nourish and cherish their wives as Christ does the church "because we are members of His body. For this reason a man shall leave his father and mother and shall be joined to his wife, and the two shall become one flesh."

Here's a theological reason that a man ought to care for his wife as his own body. The fact is that she is part of his own body. Paul said that all believers are members of Christ's body, and as such we are members of one another. This connectedness goes even deeper in marriage, because a husband and wife are part of each other in a unique way that is not true of any other human relationship.

Jesus is the perfect example for husbands, because He has so connected Himself with the church that you cannot talk about the church without talking about Jesus in the same breath, and vice versa. To put it another way, for Christ to neglect the church would be for Him to neglect Himself.

As husbands and wives we are members of each other, so that if you nourish and cherish your wife you are caring for yourself. God has joined a husband and wife together in a unique bond that unites them at every point.

CLEAVING TO YOUR WIFE

Back in Genesis 2:24, God said that it was the man's job to leave his parents and be joined to his wife. Paul quoted this principle in Ephesians 5:31 as part of his concluding instructions on marriage.

Please notice that the Bible does not say anything about a woman leaving her father and mother when she is married. Now this happens, and it's important that she do so. But the word is given to the man because it's his job as the leader in the marriage to establish something new, to sever any ties that would conflict or compete with this new relationship. A husband is to take the lead in creating an environment in which his wife can feel completely secure because she is his focus.

Besides leaving, the man is to "be joined" with his wife. The old word for this is "cleave," which means to stick like superglue in this new marriage relationship. That's what it takes for two independent, very different people to come together in a relationship that is so intimate and intense in every way that they become one flesh.

Men, it's time for you to make a declaration. As the head of your home you need to say to your wife, "I am leaving behind anything that competes with our relationship, and I am going to stick to you. I am committed to you for life, and the word 'divorce' will not come up in this house. I am going to change my strategy. Instead of complaining, I am going to start nourishing and cherishing you like the fine china you are, and I am going to become the greater servant."

Now I hope you have been given enough motivation to conduct your marriage God's way. It's the command of His Word, and it's in your best interest. But just in case you need further encouragement to be a godly husband, look again at the closing phrase of 1 Peter 3:7. It says, "So that your prayers will not be hindered."

> AS HUSBANDS AND WIVES WE ARE MEMBERS OF EACH OTHER, SO THAT IF YOU NOURISH AND CHERISH YOUR WIFE YOU ARE CARING FOR YOURSELF.

This is addressed to husbands. God says don't bother getting on your knees and crying out to Him about your needs if you are neglecting your wife's needs. Why the close connection? Because a husband and wife are members of each other, and God now deals with you on the basis of this relationship. That can be hard to get used to, but the fact is that you need to start living in line with this new reality.

The story is told of a country in which the custom many years ago was that a man had to pay his future wife's father in cows for her hand.

A man in this country had two daughters. One was young and beautiful, and the other was older and haggard looking. The father heard that a rich man in town was coming to select a wife from among his daughters and was bringing his cows with him. The father smiled inwardly as he thought of the high price that his young, beautiful daughter would bring, for he had no doubt that the rich man would choose her.

So the rich man came bringing ten cows, which was far above any amount that had ever been paid for a bride in that place. The father told his younger daughter to get herself ready, but to everyone's surprise the man chose the older, very plain daughter and paid her father ten cows for her.

Some time later, the father went to visit his daughter and her husband, and he was amazed at what he saw. This was not the haggard daughter he had given away. She was beautiful and radiant. When he asked her what had happened, she said, "When I saw how much I was valued in the eyes of my husband, I decided to start looking and acting like a ten-cow woman."

TRUSTING GOD FOR WHAT YOU NEED

I want to share a very important and encouraging closing word with you. You may have read this booklet and said to yourself, "This is all fine and good for other people who have normal marriage relationships. But no one knows the situation I have to live with in my marriage."

If this is true for you, let me tell you about a family named Evans. My father, Arthur Evans, got saved as an adult. For more than a year, he regularly got up in the early hours of the morning and went downstairs in our house in Baltimore to cry out and wail in prayer for the salvation of his wife.

And for that same year or so, my mother decided to make this man's life a living hell. She did everything she could to break him. But one morning, she came downstairs and said to my father, "What you have is real, and I want it." My father led my mother to Christ, and they led me and my siblings to Christ.

I am in the ministry today because my father decided to trust God for the needs of his family and be a faithful, godly husband whatever the cost. And I'm here to tell you that what God did for our family, He can do for yours.

You see, it's not just about your ability to meet your wife's needs. God asks you to be faithful, and He will supply what you lack. You have a Provider in heaven who will minister grace to you where grace is needed.

So before you think about throwing in the towel on

your marriage, begin nourishing and cherishing your wife and watch what happens. In fact, I challenge you to invest the next ninety days in becoming your wife's satisfier. When the service becomes that good, you'll find your wife wanting to return the favor.

THE URBAN ALTERNATIVE

THE PHILOSOPHY

Dr. Tony Evans and The Urban Alternative (TUA) **equips, empowers,** and **unites** Christians to **impact** *individuals, families, churches,* and *communities* for rebuilding lives from the inside out.

We believe the core cause of the problems we face in our personal lives, homes, and societies is a spiritual one; therefore, the only way to address them is spiritually. We've tried a political, social, economic, and even a religious agenda. It's time for a Kingdom Agenda—God's visible and comprehensive rule over every area of life.

THE PURPOSE

TUA ministers to *a world in chaos* with the goal of restoring *every area of life* to its *divine order* under the rule of God. When each biblical sphere of life functions in accordance with God's Word, the net results are an evangelized and discipled people. As people learn how to govern themselves under God, they then transform the institutions of family, church, and society from a biblically based kingdom perspective.

THE PROGRAMS

To achieve our goal we use a variety of strategies, methods, and resources for reaching and equipping as many people as possible.

• *Broadcast Media*

Millions of individuals experience *The Alternative with Dr. Tony Evans* through the daily radio broadcast playing on more than **600 stations** and in more than **40 countries**. The broadcast can also be seen on several television networks, and is viewable online through the Internet at www.tonyevans.tv.

• *Leadership Training*

The Kingdom Agenda Conference *progressively develops* churches to meet the demands of the 21st century while maintaining the Gospel message and the strategic position of the church. The conference introduces *intensive seminars, workshops,* and *resources,* addressing issues affecting

>Community
>Family
>Leadership
>Organizational Health and Growth
>Ministry Programs
>Theology, Bible, and more.

Pastors' Wives Ministry, founded by Dr. Lois Evans, provides *counsel, encouragement,* and *spiritual resources* for pastors' wives as they serve with their husbands in the ministry. A primary focus of the ministry is the **First Lady Conference** that offers senior pastors' wives a safe place to *reflect, renew,* and *relax* along with training in personal development, spiritual growth, and care for their emotional and physical well-being.

The Kingdom Agenda Fellowship of Churches (KAFOC) provides a *viable network* for *like-minded pastors* who embrace the **Kingdom Agenda** philosophy. Pastors have the opportunity to *go deeper with Dr. Tony Evans* as they are given greater biblical knowledge and practical applications and resources to impact individuals, families, churches, and communities. KAFOC welcomes *senior and associate pastors* of churches regardless of size, denominational affiliation, or race.

National Church Adopt-A-School Initiative (NCAASI) prepares churches across the country to impact communities by using *public schools as the primary vehicle for effecting positive social change* in urban youth and families. Leaders of churches, school districts, and faith-based and other nonprofit organizations are equipped with the knowledge and tools to *forge partnerships* and build *strong social service delivery systems.*

• *Resource Development*
We are fostering lifelong learning partnerships with the people we serve by providing a variety of published materials. We offer books, audiotapes, videos, and booklets to strengthen

people in their walk with God and ministry to others.

• *Outreach Model*

The Turn•Around Agenda (formerly Project Turn•Around)
TTA is a comprehensive church-based community impact strategy. It addresses such areas as economic development, education, housing, health revitalization, family renewal, and reconciliation. To model the success of the project, TUA invests in its own program locally. We also assist churches in tailoring the model to meet the specific needs of their communities, while simultaneously addressing the spiritual and moral frame of reference.

For more information, a catalog of Dr. Tony Evans'
ministry resources, and a complimentary copy of
Dr. Evans' devotional magazine,
call (800) 800-3222
or write TUA at P.O. Box 4000, Dallas TX 75208
or log on to TonyEvans.org